Always Accept Me for Who I Am

Always Accept Me for Who I Am

Instructions from Teenagers
on Raising the Perfect Parent

by

147 Teens Who Know
WILLOUGHBY-EASTLAKE
PUBLIC LIBRARY

COMPILED BY J. S. SALT

Three Rivers Press

To Miller

Copyright © 1999 by J. S. Salt

All rights reserved. No part of this book may be reproduced or transmitted in any form or
by any means, electronic or mechanical, including photocopying, recording, or by any information
storage and retrieval system, without permission in writing from the publisher.

Published by Three Rivers Press, 201 East 50th Street, New York, New York 10022.
Member of the Crown Publishing Group.

Random House, Inc. New York, Toronto, London, Sydney, Auckland
www.randomhouse.com

THREE RIVERS PRESS is a registered trademark of Random House, Inc.

DESIGN BY KAREN MINSTER

Printed in the United States of America

Library of Congress Cataloging-in-Publication Data
Always accept me for who I am : instructions from teenagers on raising the perfect parent / by 147 teens who know ;
compiled by J. S. Salt.
1. Parent and teenager—Miscellanea. 2. Parenting—Miscellanea. 3. Teenagers—Quotations. I. Salt, J. S.
HQ799.15.A45   1999   649'.125—dc21   98-50829

ISBN 0-609-80395-6

10 9 8 7 6 5 4 3 2 1

First Edition

Contents

Acknowledgments 6
Introduction 8

Support 11

Communication 35

Trust and Acceptance 63

Love and Family 103

Acknowledgments

For inviting me into their classrooms, thanks to the following schools, teachers, and administrators:

Brentwood School: Lynette Creasy and Pam Davis.

Oakwood School: Julia Coley and Rebecca Figueroa.

Parkman Middle School: Trish Horton and Susan Spica.

St. Bernard's High School: Jennifer Annick and Matthew Mallen.

Taft High School: Bridget Brownell, Nancy Cornell, Michael Jackson, Lynda Markham, Geri Siener, and Jan Stewart.

Thoreau Continuation High School: Gail Nettels and Ann Tash.

University High School: Alexa Maxwell.

Venice High School: Lynn Sabin.

For their help and support, thanks to Karen Bachrach, Carol Barring, Julie Bennett, Jim Blackwood, Deborah Bucksbaum, Charles Carney, Patty Ecker, Dr. David Feinberg, Dossie Gilbert, Julie Girocco, Russell Grossman, Kimberly D. Harold, Jonathan Harris, Laura Lee Hughes and the Unusual Suspects, Vicki and Andrew Kipper, Tracie Porter, Chris Richard, Lita Weissman, Ellen and David Wohlstadter, and Linda Zimring.

For his artistic vision, thanks to Allen Helbig.

For her unwavering support, thanks to Jessica Schulte.

And for fearlessly contributing their work and time, my greatest appreciation to the more than one thousand teens who graciously let me into their lives.

Introduction

"I'm desperate for help."

"Ever since my child turned thirteen, I have not had a moment's peace."

"Won't someone help me before I lose my mind?"

While working to promote *Always Kiss Me Good Night*, a book that featured parenting advice from kids ages six to twelve, I kept hearing those and similar pleas from parents with teens. How, as one parent complained, can we cope with these "strangers in our house" who "up to age twelve or so seemed so sweet and just about perfect"?

Accepting the challenge of those 911 calls for help, I met — over the course of a year — with more than one thousand teens from a wide variety of ethnic and economic backgrounds. We talked and shared and I invited them to write "instructions" to their parents — suggestions for improving the "quality of life" for everyone involved.

After all, it's not just the parents who suffer. Think back to your own life as a teen and see if you don't agree with poet John Ciardi: "Adolescence is enough suffering for anyone."

What we all need — parents and teens alike — is guidance, support, and improved communication during these turbulent, vexing, sanity-challenging teenage years.

Look no further than the book you now hold in your hands. Here for the taking are the insights and answers we've all been searching for. May the wit, wisdom, and sometimes anguish of these brave souls — representative of teenagers everywhere — not only remind us of what it was like "way back when" but also help guide us toward a more peaceful coexistence.

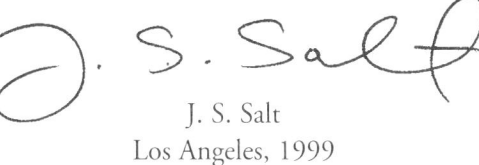

J. S. Salt
Los Angeles, 1999

Support

A little support would help my confidence. Stop looking at my negative side and start seeing the more positive me.

Sulmaz, 18

When we do something right
be proud of us. When we make
a mistake don't make it
sound like we're always wrong.

Angelina 14

Show me the way, not only through what you *DID* that was great, but also by the mistakes which have devastated you.

Michael

Age — 13

Never try to put your children down and make them feel bad, but instead encourage them in whatever they do.

Austin, 13

Expect me to win and not lose.

— Bobby, 16

I need your support when I make decisions, even if you don't agree with me.

Nancy, 13

Support me even when you know it will fail. You may be surprised with what happens.

Sam, 15

Raise me to be proud of who I am, to be a self confident & valuable person.

Elizabeth!
Age: 13

Be there when I need you, not just when it's convenient for you. I need your support during my problem from beginning to end. It's like we're married; When you have me I'm yours, you're mine. — Nathan, 17

Mom, if you would support me in my interests instead of discouraging me maybe we would have a better relationship.

Danny, age 17

Dad, you need to be more in tune to my life. I do huge projects and you don't even know they were assigned. Now you want input on where I should go to high school but how do you know what would be good for me in the next four years if you don't know what I'm doing now?

                Gina, 14

I would love it if whenever I have a personal problem I could hit a switch that turns you into a friend who's always looking out for me and who I can trust with a secret.

Eric, 17

Friend

Help me learn from my mistakes instead of throwing them in my face all of the time.

    Danita, 18

Acknowledge my accomplishments.

    Alison, 15

Support my dreams and ambitions instead of praying that I'll live up to yours.

Erika 13 years old

Complement my artwork like it's truly important.

Erin
AGE: 13

> Be open to new ideas...
> If you're wrong admit it.

Max 14

Help me earn good grades so I can get a good job and earn a lot of money. So I can have a big house and not worry about rent or paying the electricity.

Benny
age 13½

If you don't like my grades
you need to incourage me
and help me with my work,
not trip about it and yell
at me.

        Oscar, 14

I wish you would care about me more than you care about my school work and S.A.T.'s.

— Robert
15

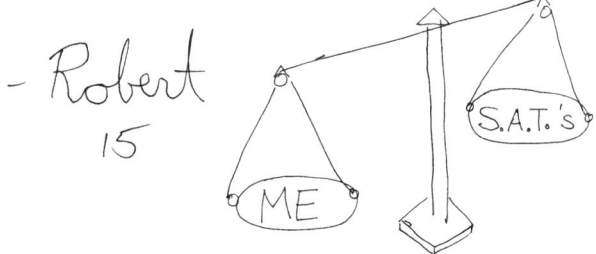

Don't pressure me so much on the future while I'm still trying to figure out the present.

Alex – 16

Don't try to fix things all the time... just be there for me.

Rebecca, 17

Dont push anything too much on your children. If your child wants to pursue something, it should be because it is their dream, not something the mother or father missed out on as children.

— Carolyn Ko

Hold my hand when
the big waves come.

Alexa (age 13)

Communication

I wish you'd listen more to all that I say. It's like my opinion doesn't matter. and it does.

        Barbara 16

Always listen to me, no matter how busy you are. Having an open ear tells me you have an open heart.

> Jessica, 15

I need to feel that I can tell you everything, even my secrets, without you barking at me.

> Nancy, 13

If you want me to explain, let me explain. Don't tell me to explain myself then tell me to shut up when I try to.

   Jeffrey, 16

I would learn more if you could explain how I am right or wrong. I am over the age now where I can just accept a plain yes or no. I need details!!

Aliza
Age: 14

I CAN'T DEAL WITH THE FACT THAT WHAT YOU ALWAYS SAY IS RIGHT AND I'm ALWAYS WRONG. IF you took some TIME AND LISTENED TO ME, YOU COULD PROBABLY GET my POINT BECAUSE IT HAS HAPPENED BEFORE.

DANIEL
16

Talk to me In a calm manner because I tend to listen better when It's not screamed Into my head.

Bryan

Age: 17

More soft talking and less yelling because that's where the Anger And arguments starts.

David
14 years old

When I am constantly being told "You stupid moron, why are you doing that?" or being called every name in the book it doesn't hurt me anymore because I know they're just words and words can't hurt you unless you let them.

Jason — 17

Be careful with words.
Words can wound and leave
scars that last a lifetime.

                Angelica
                    17

Be more open about your feelings
so I can be more open about
mine.

          Amy, 15

Don't try to protect me by keeping me in the dark so much. I know and understand more than you think.

Deboura Age: 17

Be more open with me on adult subjects so I can be more open with you.

Don
18 years Old

Communicate with me about topics like "sex" because ~~they~~ you think I don't know anything about it. An example of this is when a movie has a sex scene you expect me to shut my eyes or leave the room so I won't find out about these things. You never talk about it and if it does come ~~to~~ to mind you change the subject as fast as you can.

√ Age = 17

Tell me about yourself and your mistakes so I don't feel so tiny in your presence.

                Elaine, 14

Listen more often & maybe you won't have to ask.

      Nick, 15   *(I didn't know that!)*

Don't start asking me a hundred questions about my day the second I come home. Give me some time to decompress.

Andrew — 15

If you want to tell me to do my homework or feed the dog, just tell me. Don't keep going on about it because I don't have short term memory loss. It's when you keep telling me again and again that I start to yell and you get mad.

Rosemary, 15

Hey, Mom, you seem to think I should tell you everything that's happening in my life. I won't, ever. Get over it. Believe me, if I absolutely need to tell you, you'll be the first to know.

Stephen, Age 15

Listen more to what I have to say and let me finish what I'm saying before you put in your input.

>Rimarria
>Age 15

Try not to make every comment a lecture about life.

>David — 15

Stop telling me if I don't do good in school I'm going to be a $5.15 doller waitris and live in a $100 a month apartment. And you need to stop giving me lectures about drugs and sex 5 times a day.
Just love me.

Melissa, 14

Don't keep saying "Do as I say not as I do," Like it or not, I learn from what you ~~DO~~!!

NIKO
AGE: 14

Don't be a hypocrite. Don't tell me not to cuss, then go and cuss when you're mad!

Marcus
AGE: 14

Listen to my problems instead of getting mad before I finish my conversation.

Keverly, 14.

Try to listen to my side of the story before you blame me — because I'm the oldest.

Alexis
Age: 14

Give everybody a chance to tell a story if something went wrong and give everybody an equal chance.

Alan
AGE: 13

Don't insist, "_It_'s time to have a serious talk." Talk to me about serious things but don't make a Big Deal about it.
—Joel, 17

Spend more time with me, even if it's just sitting in a coffee shop sometime and talking about our lives.
Deborah
16

Come and talk to me when you're worried about me, because I can clear things up. And don't be upset if there are some things that I don't want you to know about my life. You're my parent, not my friend. And there's ~~s~~ nothing wrong with that.

        Lauren 15

If you would listen, you would have a chance to meet the real me.

Claudia
Age 17

Don't worry so much if you don't have the answer to a question I may have. Just keep helping me find those answers.

                Charlene, 17

The best way to talk is to have a nice hot cup of camemill tea and just see what happens.

      Elyas, 13

Trust and Acceptance

Don't listen in on my phone conversations.

Melanie — 13

Trust *me*! Don't ever judge me by things other people my age do.

Nancy, 16

Trust me with more responsibilities, and realize if I mess up on something it's my job to fix it.

Ryan 13

Go easy on me when I do something wrong.
   People make mistakes and there's a first time for everything
   You probably made mistakes when you were young.

Veronica — 13

Put your trust in me even after I broke it.

    Riana, 18

Give me some space. If I want to stay home on a weekend, don't think I'm weird.

  Angie, age 14

Don't be offended when I want to spend time with my friends. I'm just getting older and want to spend time with people my own age. I still want to be your friend (and for you to be my parents) but not all the time.

        Jason 13

Maybe if you stopped saying my cousin is the best person I would stop hating you so much.

R
age: 14

Try to understand that just because I'm different from you doesn't mean I'm bad. I don't know how I got into this family but I'm trying my best not to upset you.

Stewart, age 16

Try not to keep saying, "I can't let you do that because you'd be making the biggest mistake of your life." Everything I want to do can't be THAT earth shattering.

     Mandy, age 14

Freedom, yet not too much.
Restrictions, yet not too much.

    Helen, Age: 18

You should give me a curfew.
You're so liberal all I have to do
is call before I come home, whether
it's 10 o'clock or 2 in the morning.
You should be more strict.

Lisa, 18

MOMMA, I GET AWAY WITH MURDER. YOU NEED TO BE MORE STRICT WITH ME. YOU TELL ME I'M IN TROUBLE BUT YOU DON'T DO ANYTHING. I COULD KILL SOMEBODY AND IF YOU WERE THE JUDGE I BET I'D GET AWAY WITH IT.

JUAN, 16

Don't just give in because you're tired of hearing me. When you do, I learn how to manipulate you and get what I want. You will then lose control.

Banafsheh
15 years old

You both keep claiming you already came back from where I'm about to go. I understand your concern comes from a good place, but let me experience failure and success my own way. Give me the freedom to learn from my _OWN_ mistakes.

Doug — 17

Stop constantly telling me what not to do and I won't have to rebel. If you deprive me of my freedom you will be the one locked in the dungeon!

Yvonne
17

The more BOUNDARIES you put on me, the more REBELLIOUS I will get.

Nick, 15

Be a little more mellow with me. If you don't. some day I might snap.

Carlos
age 18

Never condescend to me and <u>Never</u> insult me —— I insult myself enough.

Matthew 15

Let me spend more time with my friends.

Jonathan
13 yrs. old

I would like to get a job and pay for things instead of your giving me money and controlling how I should spend it.

Alex, 18

DON'T THREATEN ME WHEN I MAKE MISTAKES. I'M A TEENAGER. I'M SUPPOSED TO MAKE MISTAKES.

JEFF, 14

Dad stop having a heartatack about little iddy biddy things. Just yesterday, I broke a glass and you tripped like crazy "In my years I never broke a single glass, blah, blah, blah, nag, nag, nag" GOSH. It's just a glass.

T. 17

Stop getting mad at
little things and get
mad about major Things.

    Danita, 18

PAY ATTENTION TO MY LIFE.
NOT JUST WHEN I GET IN TROUBLE!

  SAM, 17

Accept the fact that I am growing up and I need to explore the world with and without you. Put some of your fears behind you and let me take chances that are healthy for me. I can't always be right by your side and under your wing. I need to learn how to be a good leader to myself.

Trisha, 16

Look inside yourselves. Try to remember what it was like to be a teenager, maybe even relive the past. I know it might not be easy, but it will help you to understand why I make mistakes and why we have so many arguments.

Alba, 14

I wish you guys would take my music more seriously, because I like to sing and play the guitar and you don't seem like you really care. I mean, you listen to me, but you don't actually hear what my words mean when I say them. It's like when I'm talking. You look at me, but you don't really pay attention.

                Rebecca, 13

I just want you to be proud of me at least one day. That's all I want. For you guys to say "yeah my daughter she made us proud." Just for once, not compare me to my sister.

        C.   Age = 17

(speech bubbles: "that's my daughter!" — "I'm proud")

me   MOM   Dad

Let boys call my house. Then I wouldn't have to sneek around and keep things from you. Also we'd probably be more close because I would tell you everything and I wouldn't be afraid.

    Monica
    14 yrs.

So what if a guy calls me. It's not like I'm going to marry him!

    Alice, 14

MOM, never, ever tell your friend's son that I like him.

           Kenia
           AGE: 13

Don't criticize my friends when you don't even know them. And don't try to tell me who I shouldn't be friends with.

           Ana 15

I hate it when you're breathing down my neck wanting to know my every move. If you want to know what I'm really doing you should loosen up and be my friend instead of being my enemy.

Kiana, 15

If you say "Why can't you be more like your sister" one more time I think I'll explode. I can't be more like her simply because I'm **ME**, myself, and that's who I am always going to be.

As your child, I would appreciate it if you accepted me.

Nancy, 15

Don't compare me to my friends or your friends children. I'm <u>me</u>. Accept that fact and love <u>me</u> as just <u>me</u>.

Maggie
14

I need to be perceived as an <u>individualist</u>, not as a robot. By holding onto an image of what you want me to be you are closing your ears to the truth.

Dan
17

Once, just for 30 minutes, sit down and watch a whole episode of my favorite T.V. show and only then say whether it is a stupid show or not.

Rich 14

I wish you'd trust me more than you do. I don't drink. I don't smoke or do drugs and I get decent grades in school. So I don't do the dishes perfectly? So what!

I'm not saying I'm an angel, but you forget how good I am, and tend to overlook my accomplishments. There are a lot worse kids out there and I am tired of being treated like I'm a juvenile delinquent.

                Michael, age → 17

How do you not see me? I am not the perfect soul you picture in your mind. I am not the angel that won't drink or lie or be mean. Do you really know what I am doing? And if you did would you still trust me? I drink, but don't do drugs. But I don't know whether that's okay with you. Talk to me. I want to be able to tell you everything I do and not have your eyes turn down in disapointment.

Katie, 17

Let me slack off every now and then without being disappointed in me or nagging me about my work. I don't want to spend my every waking minute studying and trying to get into a good college. I want to be irresponsible sometimes. I want to have fun. I don't want to be 30 and look back and say, "Gee, I really had no life."

Elizabeth, age 14

On my last report card I got 4 A's + 2 B's. I said to you, "Guess what mom, I got 4 A's + 2 B's!" The first thing you said to me was "What'd you get the B's in?" I thought to myself, "Thanks mom, thanks for saying good job!"

                                      Jenny   Age 13

If you don't expect perfection all the time,
you won't be disappointed all the time.

                Josh age 16

Try not to hate the things that
I like, Because sooner or
later I'll grow out of it.

        Ruslan
        AGE: 16½

I am a smart and responsible person and it's about time that you believed in who I am. Know that you have raised me right and that now it's my turn to show you I can make my own decisions, that I can do things on my own.

                              Lauren 15

I'm not that embarrassed by you and I don't want to change you. What's kind of scary is that I will probably be the same kind of parent to my kids as you are to me.

        Sarah, 16

Love and Family

Leave work problems at work and come to the house happy, and happy to be with your family. You only have a family once.

Argelia
Age - 18

LET GO OF YOUR WATCH
AND YOUR CELLULAR PHONE
AND LIVE!

BRYAN
AGE: 15

Dad, spend more time with me instead of playing so much golf. And mom, be home more cause I hate the fact that you work so much!

Anna
age: 13

me by myself

Mom, You need to stop being on the phone so much and come and talk to us. Dad you need to come home earlier so you could eat dinner with us.

        Chris ; 13

I love it when you watch a movie with me. It's such a good feeling knowing that you want me to be with you. Sometimes I don't think you want to be around me, but when you sit with me and give me a hug your love runs right through me.

Will
16

Stop coming to the couch and grabbing the controller when I'm in the middle of a show because it really makes me want to scream.

Harris
Age: 15

Let me put the posters
I want in my room.

Ellen
Age: 13

Let me clean my room only when
I want to. You always tell me to
clean the room when I'm in a really
horrible mood.

Lucy
Age: 14

Give me some privacy. You're always looking through my stuff.

Esther, 14

Don't throw my things out while I'm at school.

Maria, 14

Give me an opportunity to voice my opinions in making family decisions (because usually my ideas are ignored or not considered seriously).

                Denise   14

Have a family night where our whole family can just talk and bond and share our feelings. — Glenn, 15

I know you won't be around forever so lets do more things together like go on vacations and trips to semi-close towns.

     Jenana, Age 13

Boys need to do more things with their dads. Go out together, bond, and have fun together.

   Will
   16

Dad, I love spending time with you, even if it's for a couple of minutes or hours. Maybe you could take some time off from work and we could do something. Maybe a fishing trip or a basketball game.

Eric
14 years old

Mom, I want to have little parties together and put makeup on eachother, paint our nails over a bag of popcorn and talk about guys, not just say, "I'm too old for that stuff, honey."

                         Michelle
                         14

I like it when you people watch with me:

"Check out that guy with his belly hanging out."

"Wow, that couple has a lot of children."

"Oh my god, what is that person wearing???"

These are just a few of the questions my Mother and I furtively whisper to one another on a Saturday afternoon.

We all do have our forms of entertainment!

Jessica, age 13

I Love it when my mom ceresses
my face and tells me I'm growing
up beautifuly and I also Love
how she makes me laugh,
even when I'm mad and I
don't want to laugh.

    Erin
    AGE: 13

I Love it when You...
Make me feel Secure & Loved
Unconditionally.

I hate it when You...
Give me the cold shoulder.

Doug, 16

When I bring friends over, don't try to impress them. Just say hi!, and let us go on our way.

        Kenia
        AGE 13

Mom, I wish you wouldn't yell at me about irrelevant things in front of my friends.

        Jill 16 years

I wish my mom didn't smoke because now I smoke and if I wanted to stop it would be complicated because it's in my household.

Kamelia   18 yrs. old

Dad what I needed was a little more attention and interest in my life beyond the one day that I brought home my report card.

　　　　　Victor
　　　　　(18)

Comming home and questioning me about every aspect of my life does not make up for the fact that you spend more time at the office than you do at the dinner table.

David/16

Instead of dropping me off at basketball practice, come and practice with me.

Edward – 14

Come to my games. Watch your creation do something I love.

JOHN, 17

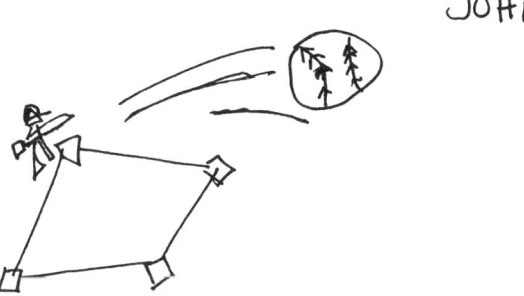

Dad, I want you to raise me <u>showing</u> me some kind of love, not just caring about ~~my~~ health and success in school.

You never talk to me about deep, personal things. You never tried to get closer to me and I don't like you for that.

Adam
14

I have never really felt that strong loving bond that a father and son share. It's a little weird because you and I don't discuss anything plus you have to consider that you are hardly at home on any given week. When you are home and I wake up you are already downstairs on your phone conversations.

Geff — 17

When we eat dinner together, either it is going to be silent or dad will comment on something wrong that I did. Ever since ninth grade, I've always had to lie my way in order to get around. That is really sad because I want parents who I could share stories with and be honest with.

                Holly 17 years.

Everyone has goodness inside of them. It just takes another person to spark it. Sort of like a chain reaction. So let me into your world and show you that I can do it.

~ Sean ~
17.

punishment and violence doesn't work. Your parents should be your role models in life and people you look up to rather then people you avoid and have to lie to in order to be able to do what you want.

J Age 17

My bedtime is at 12:00 with my Dad. At my Mom's it is 11:00. This is very hard on me so try to get your acts together.

Bryan, 14

I would like it if the two
of you could start to talk again
and not always be fighting. At
least stay like friends. That
would make the family get closer.

                         Nina 16 years

Let me see my dad more often.

Timothy – 14

California — me — I can't see you

Florida — DAD — Neither can I

Don't get mad at me when my younger brother does something wrong. I try to be an example but I can't control him anymore than you can.

Julia 17 (almost 18)

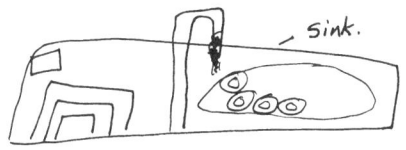

Stop pestering me to wash the dishes.
Let my brothers do the dishes sometimes.

Joyce
Age 13

Never ever play favorites with one child as opposed to another because it tears the other child apart and tends to make that child feel less significant in the world.

— Carolyn 16

Love all your children equally. Have no one get more than the other, and let no one ever feel left out.

Danny
18 years old

Stop fighting so much and fall back in love and take a vacation with just the two of you.

Ana age 13

Do more things for yourself. Go out once in a while. Start dating again.

Josh, 15

"GIVE ME SOME LOVIN' AND A WHOLE LOTTA ATTENTION!"

MARY
AGE - 17

Raise me with all the love there is to give, so when I grow up I would treat people the same way you treated me and give my own son or daughter just as much love.

Hector / 17

Worry less about how to raise me and more about how to ♡love♡ me.
♡ ♡ ♡

Laura
age 15

I'm glad you always let me know you love me no matter what. Don't ever change that.

Doug, 16